how2become

ABSTRACT REASONING TESTS

www.How2Become.com

by Richard McMunn

To help you further understand Abstract Reasoning Test Questions I have created a FREE video for you at the following page:

www.AbstractReasoning.co.uk

Get more products for passing any type of test or interview at:

www.how2become.com

Orders: Please contact How2become Ltd, Suite 3, 50 Churchill Square Business Centre, Kings Hill, Kent ME19 4YU. You can also order via the e mail address info@how2become.co.uk.

ISBN: 9781910202395

First published in 2014 by How2Become Ltd

Typeset for How2become Ltd by Anton Pshinka.

Printed in Great Britain for How2become Ltd by CMP (uk) Limited, Poole, Dorset.

CONTENTS

Introduction to your new guide 6

About abstract reasoning tests 11

Abstract reasoning tests section 1.....................................55

Abstract reasoning tests section 2 99

Abstract reasoning tests section 3.................................... 143

Abstract reasoning tests section 4 161

A few final words 224

As part of this product you have also re-ceived **FREE** access to online tests that will help you to pass abstract reasoning tests

To gain access, simply go to:

www.PsychometricTestsOnline.co.uk

INTRODUCTION TO YOUR NEW GUIDE

Dear Sir/Madam,

Welcome to your new guide, Abstract Reasoning Tests. This guide contains lots of sample test questions that are appropriate for anyone who is required to take an abstract reasoning test. The key to success in any career or job-related assessment is to try your hardest to get 100% correct answers in the test that you are undertaking. If you aim for 100% in your preparation, then you are far more likely to achieve the trade or career that you want. We have deliberately supplied you with lots of sample questions to assist you. It is crucial that when you get a question wrong, you take the time to find out why you got it wrong. Understanding the question is very important.

Finally, if you want to try out more tests that will prepare you for your assessment then we offer a wide range of products to assist you at www.how2become.com. We have also created a FREE training video that will explain further how to tackle abstract reasoning tests at the following webpage:

www.AbstractReasoning.co.uk

Good luck and best wishes,

The how2become team

The How2become team

PREFACE BY AUTHOR RICHARD MCMUNN

It's probably important that I start off by explaining a little bit about myself, my background, and also why I'm suitably qualified to help you prepare for your abstract reasoning test.

At the time of writing I am 41 years old and live in Tunbridge Wells, Kent. I left school at the usual age of 16 and joined the Royal Navy, serving on-board HMS Invincible as part of 800 Naval Air Squadron which formed part of the Fleet Air Arm. There I was, at the age of 16, travelling the world and working as an engineer on Sea Harrier jets! It was fantastic and I loved every minute of it. After four years I left the Royal Navy and joined Kent Fire and Rescue Service as a firefighter.

Over the next 17 years I worked my way up through the ranks to the position of Assistant Divisional Officer. During my time in the Fire Service I spent a lot of time working as an instructor at the Fire Brigade Training Centre. I was also involved in the selection process for assessing candidates who wanted to join the job as a firefighter. Therefore, my knowledge and experience gained so far in life has been invaluable in helping people like you to pass any type of selection process. I am sure you will find this guide an invaluable resource during your preparation for your assessment.

I have always been fortunate in the fact that I persevere at everything I do. I've understood that if I keep working hard in life then I will always be successful; or I will achieve whatever it is that I want to achieve. This is an important lesson that I want you to take on-board straight away. If you work hard and persevere, then success will come your way. It is also very important that you believe in your own abilities. It does not matter if you have no qualifications. It does not matter if are currently weak in the area of abstract reasoning or psychometric testing. What does matter is self-belief, self-discipline and a genuine desire to improve and become successful.

Finally, as part of this product I want to give you FREE access to online tests that will help you to pass abstract reasoning tests. To gain access, simply go to:

www.PsychometricTestsOnline.co.uk

Best wishes,

Richard McMunn

Richard McMunn

DISCLAIMER

Every effort has been made to ensure that the information contained within this guide is accurate at the time of publication. How2become Ltd are not responsible for anyone failing any part of any selection process as a result of the information contained within this guide. How2become Ltd and their authors cannot accept any responsibility for any errors or omissions within this guide, however caused. No responsibility for loss or damage occasioned by any person acting, or refraining from action, as a result of the material in this publication can be accepted by How2become Ltd.

The information within this guide does not represent the views of any third party service or organisation.

ABOUT ABSTRACT REASONING TESTS

Abstract Reasoning tests are being used more and more in roles that require an ability to make quick decisions in pressurised situations, such as roles within the medical profession. Abstract reasoning requires an ability to identify patterns amongst different abstract shapes where irrelevant and distracting material is often present. The presence of irrelevant or distracting material or information can sometimes lead to incorrect conclusions. Abstract reasoning tests therefore measure a candidate's ability to change track, critically evaluate and generate hypotheses and to query judgements as they progress through the test.

How long are the tests?

The time that you will be provided to sit the abstract reasoning test will very much depend on the role you are applying for. However, to give you an idea, the tests that form part of the UK clinical aptitude test last for a maximum of 14 minutes, during which time the candidate has to answer 55 questions. The tests are designed so that it is very difficult to complete them. Whilst the assessor or test centre are looking for you to complete as many test questions as possible, they are also looking for you to get the questions you have answered, correct. Therefore, during your preparation you must concentrate on speed as well as accuracy.

What do the questions look like?

Again, the type of question you will be required to tackle during the abstract reasoning test will depend on the role you are applying for. However, in order to help you prepare I will provide you with a number of sample questions and explanations which will help give you a better understanding of what you are going to be presented with during the actual test.

Sample question type 1 – determining which figure comes next in a sequence based on the options available.

In the following sample question you have to decide which figure comes next in the sequence. With this type of question you should be looking for things such as:

- Issues around size and shape of objects.
- Number of objects.
- Sides of objects.
- Shading and colour.
- Symmetry.

- Number of angles.
- Position and direction etc.

Whilst it may appear that you have to look for lots of variations when tackling this type of test you will find that the more you practice the faster you will become at finding the solution.

Q. Which figure comes next in the sequence?

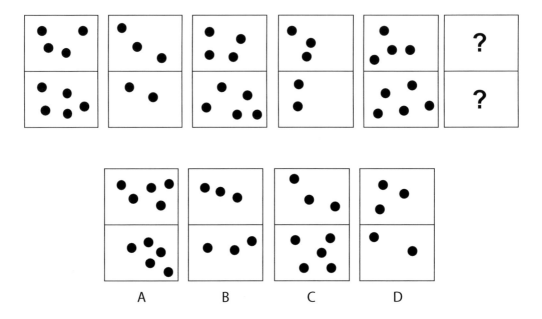

A   B   C   D

Answer: D

As the sequence progresses the number of dots alternates in opposite section of the rectangle. For example, the top of the first rectangle has 4 black dots and the bottom of the second rectangle has 2 black dots. The top of the third rectangle has 4 black dots and the bottom of the fourth has 2 black dots and so on. Conversely, the number of black dots in the bottom of the first rectangle has 5 black dots and the top of the second rectangle has 3 black dots and so on. Therefore, the correct answer is D.

So, when responding to this question we can see that it is the '**number of objects**' presented which was the main factor that we needed to observe and assess.

Let's now take a look at another sample question based on your requirement to determine which figures comes next in the sequence based on the options available.

Q. Which figure comes next in the sequence?

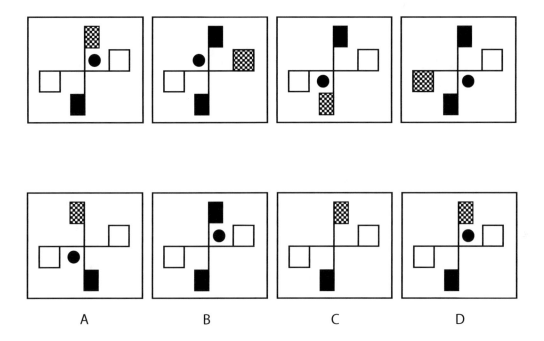

A   B   C   D

Answer: D

Throughout the duration of the sequence the figures stay in the same position. However, you will notice that one of the 'attached' shapes changes from its original colour or shade to a chequered effect as the sequence progresses before reverting back to its original colour or shade. You will also notice that chequered shape moves around the figure in a clockwise direction as the sequence progresses. In addition to this there is also a black dot within the figure which moves around the figure in an anti-clockwise manner as the sequence progresses. Therefore, the next shape in the sequence is D.

So, when responding to this question we can see that it was the **'shading and colour'** of the attached shapes and also the **'position and direction'** of the black dot presented which were the main factors that we needed to observe and assess in order to reach our answer.

As you are probably beginning to realise, abstract reasoning tests can become quite confusing and frustrating as you get deeper into the test. That is why it is so important to understand the different ways you can effectively tackle the questions quickly and accurately.

Let's now take a look at another type of abstract reasoning test question that you may come across during your actual test.

Sample question type 2 – you will be presented with two sets of shapes labelled "Set A" and "Set B". You will be given a test shape and asked to decide whether the test shape belongs to Set A, Set B, or Neither.

Q. Determine whether the test shapes belong to Set A, Set B or Neither.

Set A		Set B			Test Shape
A B J	C H U	K E D	A Z R	1	H C X
K R U	B O Z	X R L	P W A	2	K D P
S C Y	C U X	E D N	L F B	3	D U C

This question is not easy to answer, simply because you have to think outside of the box in order to achieve the correct answer. Most people who look at the question will be looking for links between the actual letters themselves, as opposed to how the letters are actually presented. You will note that each square in Set A includes one letter which includes a straight line and two letters which include curves, whereas each box of Set B contains the opposite, two letters with straight lines and one letter with a curve. Therefore, the correct answers are:

Test shape 1 belongs to Set B because it has two straight letters and one curved.

Test shape 2 belongs to Set A because it has two curved letters and one straight.

Test shape 3 belongs to neither because it has three curved letters.

So, when responding to this question we can see that it was the **'issues around size and shape of objects'** that we needed to observe and assess in order to reach our answer.

Now let's take a look at the same type of question but in a different format.

Q. Determine whether the test shapes belong to Set A, Set B or Neither.

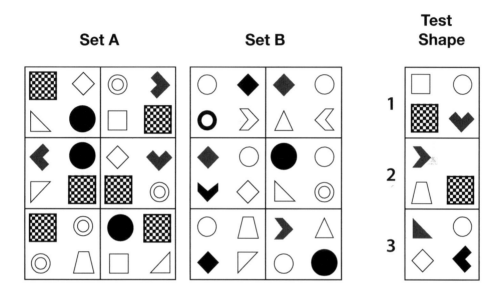

In this question we are looking for links between the sets and the test shapes. Test shape 1 does not belong to neither sets as it contains a chequered square and a white circle. You will notice that neither Set A nor Set B contain both a chequered square and a white circle. In order for test shape 1 to belong to Set A the white circle would have to change to different shape, such as a black circle.

In order for test shape 1 to belong to Set B, the chequered square and white square would both have to be replaced by different shapes, such as an arrow or white triangle.

Test shape 2 contains a chequered square which is indication that the shape may belong to Set A. Upon further investigation the other symbols in the box you can see that it does not contain a white circle, something which is prominent in every square of Set B. Therefore, test shape 2 does in fact belong to Set A.

Test shape 3 has white circle and no chequered square. Therefore, the correct answer is that test shape 3 belongs to Set B.

So, when responding to this type of question we can see that it was the **'issues around size and shape of objects'**, **'number of objects'** and **'shading and colour'** that we needed to observe and assess in order to reach our answers.

Now let's take a look at another type of abstract reasoning test question.

Sample question type 3 – you will be presented with two sets of shapes. An example is as follows:

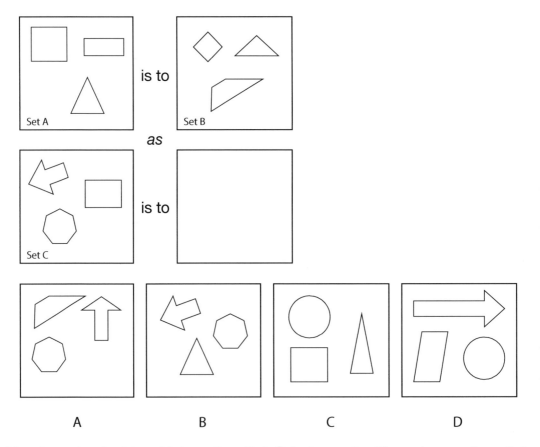

A   B   C   D

You have to decide which option Set C belongs to. There is usually a link between the different sets of shapes, so make sure you study them carefully. For example, in the above question you will notice that in both Set A and Set B there are two shapes each with 4 sides and one shape with 3 sides. In Set C there are two shapes each with 7 sides and one with 4 sides. Therefore, the correct answer is A.

So, when responding to this type of question we can see that it was the **'issues around size and shape of objects'** and the **'number of objects'** that we needed to assess and observe in order to reach our answer.

Now let's take a look at one more type of abstract reasoning test question before you progress on to the sample test sections.

Sample question type 4 – in this type of question you have to decide which figure is the odd one out.

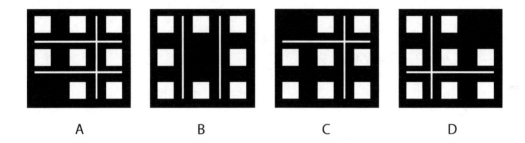

| A | B | C | D |

Whilst examining the above figures you will notice that figure A is the only one with 3 white lines and 8 white squares. All of the other figures have 2 white lines and 8 white squares.

Let's now take a look at some important additional abstract reasoning test strategies that will help you to gain higher scores during the real test.

Abstract Reasoning Strategies

» Timing is important when responding to abstract reasoning type questions. Do not spend too much time on a particular question. For example, if you are required to answer 55 questions in just 14 minutes that effectively leaves you on average just 15 seconds per question! You need to practice lots of questions to get used to answering them in a fast and accurate manner.

» Don't forget to think about issues around size and shape of objects; number of objects, sides of objects, shading and colour, symmetry, number of angles, position and direction etc.

» Questions which require you to identify which shape fits in set A or set B will often be linked in some way – remembering this may help you ignore distracting information.

There's no two ways about it, the most effective way in which you can prepare for the tests is to carry out lots of sample test questions. When I say lots, I mean lots! Before I provide you with a host of test questions for you to try, here are a few more important tips for you to consider:

- Abstract reasoning requires an ability to identify patterns amongst different abstract shapes where irrelevant and distracting material is often present. The presence of irrelevant or distracting material or information can sometimes lead to incorrect conclusions. Abstract reasoning tests therefore measure a candidate's ability to change track, critically evaluate and generate hypotheses and to query judgements as they progress through the test. The sample test questions within this guide will help you to improve in the areas of critical evaluation and judgment. Make sure you also watch the video at **www.AbstractReasoning.co.uk** as the more information there will help you understand the test questions and how to best tackle them.

- It is important that, before you sit your test, you find out the type(s) of questions you will be required to undertake. You should also take steps to find out if the tests will be timed and also whether or not they will be 'multiple-choice' based questions. If the tests that you will be required to undertake are timed and of multiple-choice in nature, then I strongly advise that you practice this type of test question.

- Variety is the key to success. I recommend that you attempt a variety of different test questions, such as psychometric tests, numerical reasoning, verbal reasoning, spatial reasoning, fault analysis and mechanical reasoning etc. This will undoubtedly improve your overall ability to pass the test that you are required to undertake. If you go to the free tests at **www.PsychometricTestsOnline.co.uk** then you will be able to try all of these free of charge. I would also recommend you obtain a copy of my 220 page spatial reasoning test questions booklet from Amazon or through How2Become.com as this book is also great additional preparation for an abstract reasoning test or assessment.

- Confidence is an important part of test preparation. Have you ever sat a timed test and your mind goes blank? This is because your mind is focused on negative thoughts and your belief that you will fail the test. If you practice plenty of test questions under timed conditions then your confidence will grow. If your confidence is at its peak at the commencement of the test then there is no doubt that you will actually look forward to sitting it, as opposed to being fearful of the outcome.

- Whilst this is a very basic tip that may appear obvious, many people neglect to follow it. Make sure that you get a good night's sleep the night before your test or assessment. Research has shown that those people who have regular 'good' sleep are far more likely to concentrate better during psychometric tests.

- Aim for SPEED as well as ACCURACY. Many test centres want to see how quickly you can work, but they also want to see how accurate your work is, too. Therefore, when tackling the tests you must work as quickly as you can without sacrificing accuracy. Most tests are designed so that you do no finish them and you will most probably lose marks for incorrect answers.

- You are what you eat! In the week prior to the test eat and drink healthily. Avoid cigarettes, alcohol and food with high fat content. The reason for this is that all of these will make you feel sluggish and you will not perform at your peak. On the morning of your assessment eat a healthy breakfast such as porridge and a banana.

- Drink plenty of water, always!

- If you have any special needs that need to be catered for ensure you inform the assessment centre staff prior to the assessment day. I have met people in the past who are fearful of telling the assessment staff that they are dyslexic. You will not be treated negatively; in fact the exact opposite. They will give you extra time in the tests which can only work in your favour.

Now that I have provided you with a number of important tips, take the time to work through the four different sample test sections that are contained within the guide. You will need a stop watch in order to assess your performance against the time constraints for each test.

ABSTRACT REASONING TEST
SECTION 1

In abstract reasoning test section 1 there are 20 questions and you have just 10 minutes to answer them

ABSTRACT REASONING TEST SECTION 1

Q1. Which SET does the TEST SHAPE belong to?

SET A	SET B	TEST SHAPE

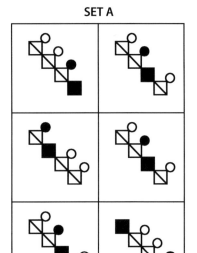 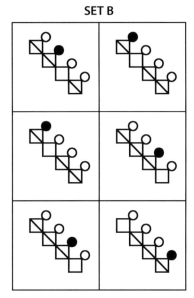 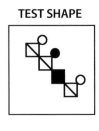

SET A   ○

SET B   ○

NEITHER   ○

Q2. Which SET does the TEST SHAPE belong to?

SET A   SET B   TEST SHAPE

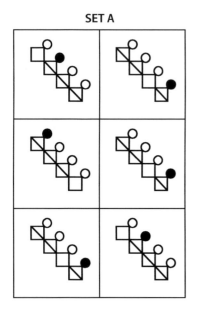 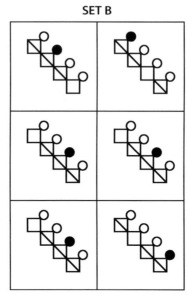 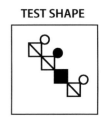

SET A ⬭

SET B ⬭

NEITHER ⬭

Q3. Which SET does the TEST SHAPE belong to?

SET A	SET B	TEST SHAPE

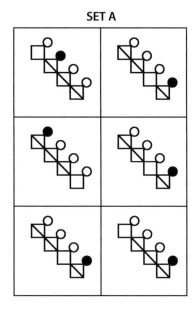 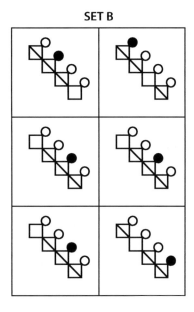 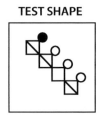

SET A ◯

SET B ◯

NEITHER ◯

Q4. Which SET does the TEST SHAPE belong to?

SET A	SET B	TEST SHAPE

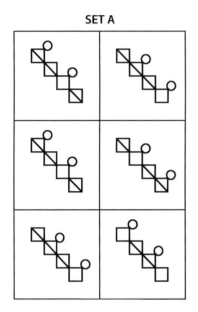 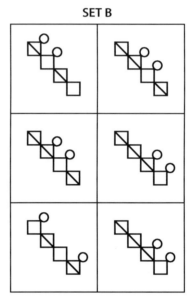 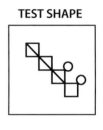

SET A ◯

SET B ◯

NEITHER ◯

Q5. Which SET does the TEST SHAPE belong to?

SET A   SET B   TEST SHAPE

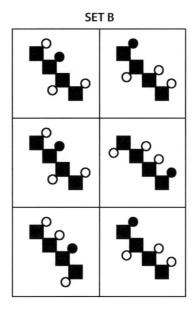 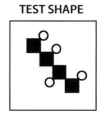

SET A   ◯

SET B   ◯

NEITHER   ◯

Q6. Which SET does the TEST SHAPE belong to?

SET A	SET B	TEST SHAPE
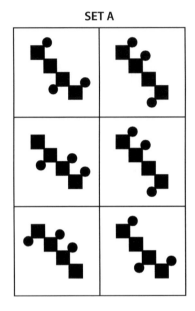	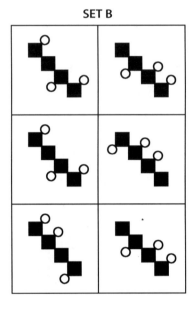	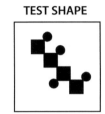

SET A ◯

SET B ◯

NEITHER ◯

Q7. Which SET does the TEST SHAPE belong to?

SET A	SET B	TEST SHAPE

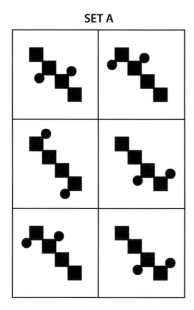 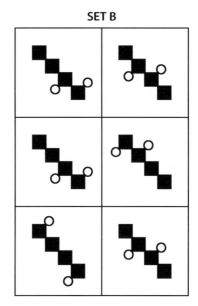 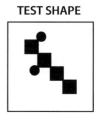

SET A   〇

SET B   〇

NEITHER   〇

Q8. Which SET does the TEST SHAPE belong to?

SET A   SET B   TEST SHAPE

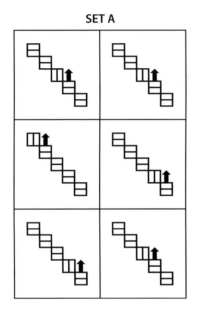 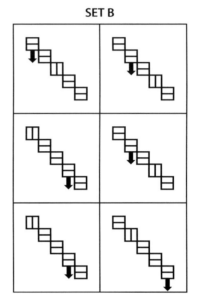 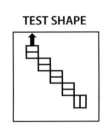

SET A   ◯

SET B   ◯

NEITHER   ◯

Q9. Which SET does the TEST SHAPE belong to?

SET A	SET B	TEST SHAPE

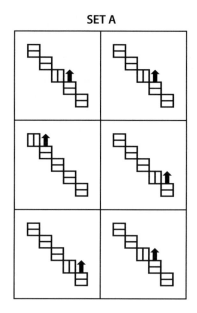

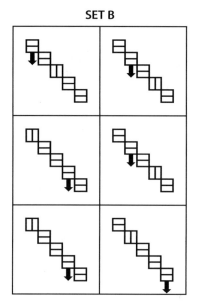

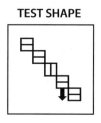

SET A ◯

SET B ◯

NEITHER ◯

Q10. Which SET does the TEST SHAPE belong to?

SET A   SET B   TEST SHAPE

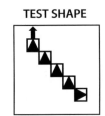

SET A   ◯

SET B   ◯

NEITHER   ◯

Q11. Which SET does the TEST SHAPE belong to?

SET A   SET B   TEST SHAPE

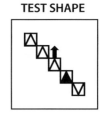

SET A   ◯

SET B   ◯

NEITHER   ◯

Q12. Which SET does the TEST SHAPE belong to?

	SET A		SET B		TEST SHAPE

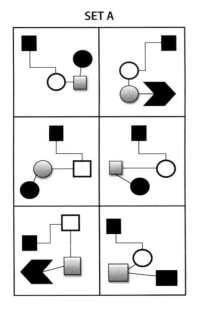 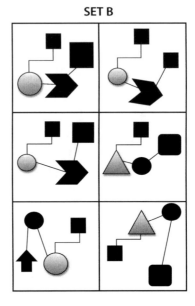 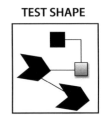

SET A ◯

SET B ◯

NEITHER ◯

Q13. Which SET does the TEST SHAPE belong to?

SET A	SET B	TEST SHAPE
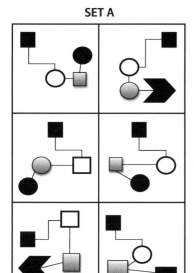	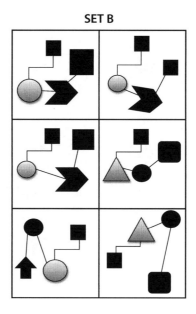	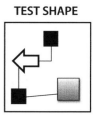

SET A ◯

SET B ◯

NEITHER ◯

Q14. Which SET does the TEST SHAPE belong to?

SET A	SET B	TEST SHAPE

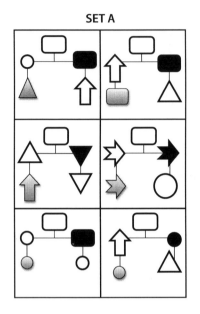 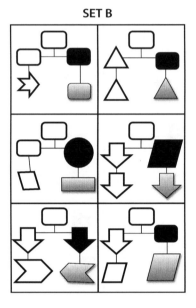 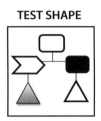

SET A ◯

SET B ◯

NEITHER ◯

Q15. Which of the 3 TEST SHAPES belongs to SET A?

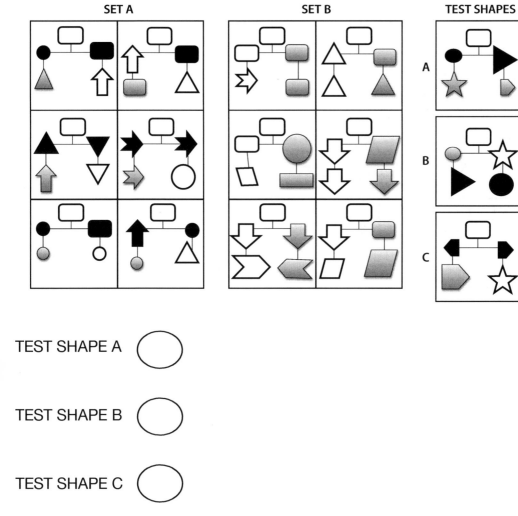

TEST SHAPE A   ◯

TEST SHAPE B   ◯

TEST SHAPE C   ◯

NEITHER   ◯

Q16. Which of the 3 TEST SHAPES belongs to SET B?

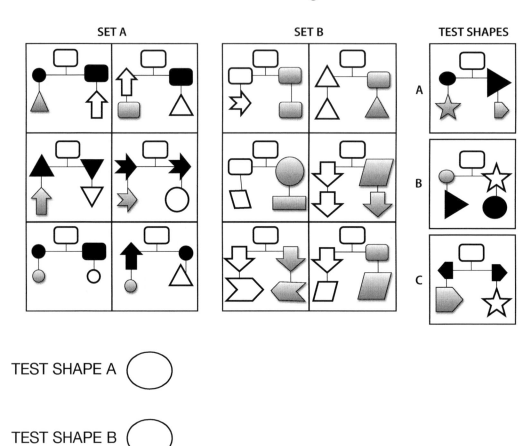

TEST SHAPE A ◯

TEST SHAPE B ◯

TEST SHAPE C ◯

NEITHER ◯

Q17. Which of the 3 TEST SHAPES belongs to SET A?

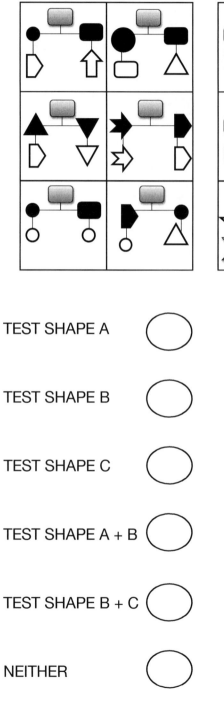

TEST SHAPE A   ◯

TEST SHAPE B   ◯

TEST SHAPE C   ◯

TEST SHAPE A + B   ◯

TEST SHAPE B + C   ◯

NEITHER   ◯

Q18. Which of the 3 TEST SHAPES belongs to SET B?

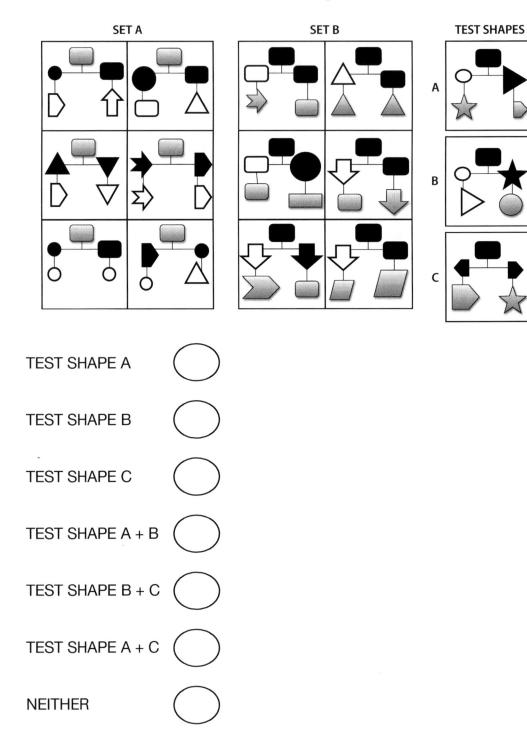

TEST SHAPE A ◯

TEST SHAPE B ◯

TEST SHAPE C ◯

TEST SHAPE A + B ◯

TEST SHAPE B + C ◯

TEST SHAPE A + C ◯

NEITHER ◯

Q19. Which of the 3 TEST SHAPES belongs to SET A?

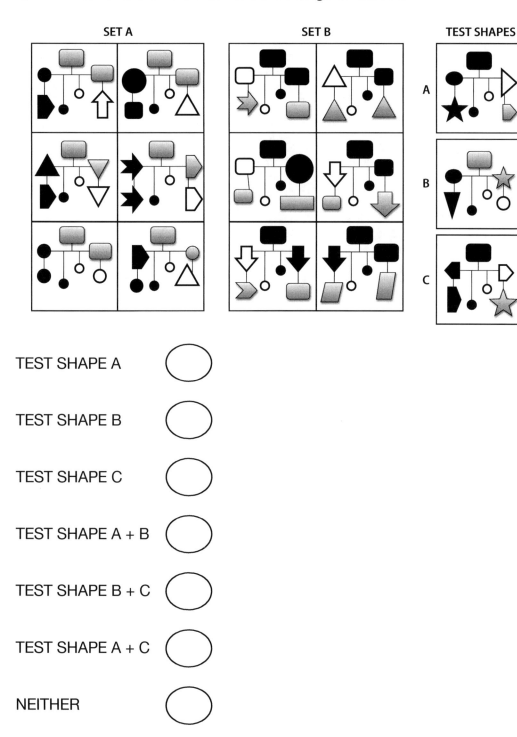

TEST SHAPE A   ○

TEST SHAPE B   ○

TEST SHAPE C   ○

TEST SHAPE A + B   ○

TEST SHAPE B + C   ○

TEST SHAPE A + C   ○

NEITHER   ○

Q20. Which of the 3 TEST SHAPES belongs to SET B?

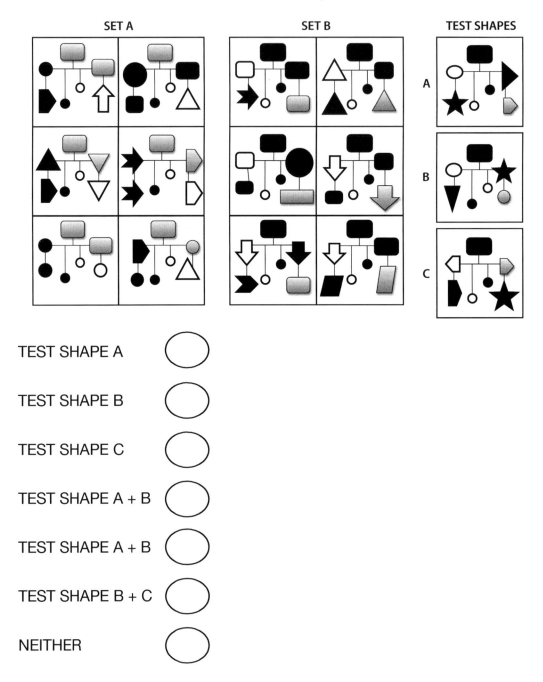

| | SET A | | SET B | | TEST SHAPES |

TEST SHAPE A ◯

TEST SHAPE B ◯

TEST SHAPE C ◯

TEST SHAPE A + B ◯

TEST SHAPE A + B ◯

TEST SHAPE B + C ◯

NEITHER ◯

Now please check your answers carefully before moving on to the next section.

ANSWERS TO ABSTRACT REASONING TEST SECTION 1

Q1. SET A

The Test Shape fits with Set A because it has 2 white dots and 1 black dot. It also has one black square and 3 squares that have diagonal lines.

SET A: There are 4 squares in a diagonal. If a square has a black dot then the following square down in the sequence is black and does not have a dot. If the last square in the sequence of 4 has a black dot the first square will be black.

SET B: There are 4 squares in a diagonal. If a square has a black dot then the following square down in the sequence does not have a line running through it. If the last square in the sequence of 4 has a black dot the first square will be the one without the line running through it.

Q2. NEITHER

The Test Shape doesn't fit in to neither. It is clear that both sets do not contain a black square and the Test Shape does, therefore doesn't belong to any set.

SET A: There are 4 squares in a diagonal. If a square has no line running through it then the next square down has a black dot. If the last square in the sequence of 4 has no line running through it then the first square will have a black dot.

SET B: There are 4 squares in a diagonal. If a square has no line running through it then the second square down from it will have a black dot. If the last square in the sequence of 4 has no line running through it then the second square from the top will have a black dot.

Q3. SET B

The Test Shape fits with Set B because the black dot is two spaces down from the square that has no line running through it, which follows the pattern of Set B.

SET A: There are 4 squares in a diagonal. If a square has no line running through it then the next square down has a black dot. If the last square in the sequence of 4 has no line running through it then the first square will have a black dot.

SET B: There are 4 squares in a diagonal. If a square has no line running through it then the second square down from it will have a black dot. If the second from last square in the sequence of 4 has no line running through it then the first square from the top will have a black dot.

Q4. SET B

The Test Shape fits with Set B because if the square has a diagonal line running through it and a white dot, the next square will have a white dot but no diagonal line in the square. The test shape follows this pattern.

SET A: There are 4 squares in a diagonal. If a square has a line running through it and a white dot then second square down from it also has a white dot but no line running through it. If the last square in the sequence of 4 is the one with a line running through it and a white dot, then the second square from the top with have a dot but no line running through it.

SET B: There are 4 squares in a diagonal. If a square has a line running through it and a white dot then the next one down from it also has a white dot but no line running through it. If the last square in the sequence of 4 is the one with a line running through it and a white dot, then the first square at the top will have a dot but no line running through it.

Q5. NEITHER

The Test Shape doesn't fit in to either Sets. In Set A contains 3 black dots and only one white. Set B contains 3 white dots and only 1 black. The Test Shape has 4 white dots, so therefore cannot fit in to either Sets.

SET A: There are 4 black squares in a diagonal. If a square has a white dot located in the top right hand corner then the next square down from it will have a black dot on the bottom left hand corner. If the last square in the sequence of 4 is the one with a white dot then the first square at the top of the sequence will be the one with a black dot on the bottom left hand corner.

SET B: There are 4 black squares in a diagonal. If a square has a black dot located in the top right hand corner then the next square down from it will have a white dot on the bottom left hand corner. If the last square in the sequence of 4 is the one with a black dot then the first square at the top of the sequence will be the one with a white dot on the bottom left hand corner.

Q6. NEITHER

The Test Shape doesn't fit in to either Sets. In Set A, it contains 3 black dots. In Set B, it contains 3 white dots. The Test Shape contains 4 black dots and therefore cannot fit in to either Sets.

SET A: There are 4 black squares in a diagonal. If a square has no dot located on the top right hand corner then the next square down from it will have a black dot on the bottom left hand corner. If the last square in the sequence of 4 is the one with no dot then the first square at the top of the sequence will be the one with a black dot on the bottom left hand corner.

SET B: There are 4 black squares in a diagonal. If a square has no dot located on the top right hand corner then the next square down from it will have a white dot on the bottom left hand corner. If the last square in the sequence of 4 is the one with no dot then the first square at the top of the sequence will be the one with a white dot on the bottom left hand corner.

Q7. NEITHER

The Test Shape doesn't fit in to either Sets. In Set A, If a shaded square has a dot on the bottom left corner, then the next shaded square will have a dot on the top right corner. In Set B, the same thing is happening as seen in Set A, except they are white dots instead of black. The Test shape shows if the square has a dot on the top right corner, then the next square will have a dot on the bottom left corner.

SET A: There are 4 black squares in a diagonal. If a square has a black dot located on the bottom left hand corner then the next square down from it will have a black dot on the top right hand corner. If the last square in the sequence of 4 is the one with a black dot on the bottom left hand corner then the first square at the top of the sequence will be the one with a black dot on the right hand corner.

SET B: There are 4 black squares in a diagonal. If a square has a white dot located on the bottom left hand corner then the next square down from it will have a white dot on the top right hand corner. If the last square in the sequence of 4 is the one with a white dot in the bottom left hand corner then the first square at the top of the sequence will be the one with a white dot in the right hand corner.

Q8. SET A

The Test Shape fits with Set A. The first vertical square in the sequence means the next square will have an arrow pointing upwards. In the Test Shape, the vertical square is the last in the sequence, so the arrow will be placed at the start of the sequence.

SET A: There are 5 white squares in a diagonal. If a square has a vertical line running through it then the next square will have a black arrow pointing upwards. If the last square in the sequence of 5 is the one with a vertical line running though it then the first square at the top of the sequence will be the one with an arrow pointing upwards.

SET B: There are 5 white squares in a diagonal. If a square has an arrow pointing downwards then the second square that follows in the sequence will have a vertical line running through it. If the second to last square in the sequence of 5 is the one with an arrow pointing downwards then the first square at the top of the sequence will be the one with a vertical line running through it.

Q9. NEITHER

The Test Shapes doesn't fit in to neither Sets. It cannot fit in to Set A because the arrows are pointing up and in the Test Shape, they are pointing down. In Set B, there are four consecutive squares that have horizontal lines, the arrow is placed on the third square. However, the Test Shape places the arrow on the first square that has a horizontal line.

SET A: There are 5 white squares in a diagonal. If a square has a vertical line running through it then the next square will have a black arrow pointing upwards. If the last square in the sequence of 5 is the one with a vertical line running though it then the first square at the top of the sequence will be the one with an arrow pointing upwards.

SET B: There are 5 white squares in a diagonal. If a square has an arrow pointing downwards then the second square that follows in the sequence will have a vertical line running through it. If the second to last square in the sequence of 5 is the one with an arrow pointing downwards then the first square at the top of the sequence will be the one with a vertical line running through it.

Q10. SET B

The Test Shape fits with Set B. If the triangle in the square is pointing to the right, than the next square will have an arrow pointing upwards. It cannot fit into Set A because the arrow is placed above the square that has the triangle pointing to the right.

SET A: There are 5 white squares in a diagonal. If a square has an arrow standing on top of it, then the next square in the sequence will have a triangle pointing to the right inside it. If the last square in the sequence of 5 is the an arrow standing on top of it, then the first square in the sequence will be the one with a triangle pointing to the right inside it.

SET B: There are 5 white squares in a diagonal. If a square has a triangle pointing to the right inside it, then the next square in the sequence will have an arrow standing on top of it. If the last square in the sequence of 5 is the one a triangle pointing to the right inside it, then the first square in the sequence will be the one with an arrow standing on top of it.

Q11. NEITHER

The Test Shape doesn't fit in to neither sets. The Test Shape shows that the arrow is placed on the square above the one with the black triangle. Neither Set A nor B shows the same pattern and therefore cannot belong to either sets.

SET A: There are 5 squares in a diagonal. If a square has a black triangle inside it, then the next square in the sequence will have an inverted triangle inside it. Two squares further down the sequence from the inverted triangle there will be a square with a white triangle with a black arrow sitting on top of the square. If the last square in the sequence of 5 is the one with the black triangle, then the first square in the sequence will be the one with an inverted triangle inside it.

SET B: There are 5 squares in a diagonal. If a square has a black triangle inside it, then the second square in the sequence following it will have an inverted triangle inside it. One squares further down the sequence from the inverted triangle there will be a square with a white triangle with a black arrow sitting on top of the square. If the last square in the sequence of 5 is the one with the black triangle, then the second square in the sequence from the top will be the one with an inverted triangle inside it.

Q12. SET B

The Test Shape belongs to Set B because the pattern starts with a black shape which links to a grey shaded shape, to another black shape and then another black shape. The Test Shape has the same pattern as Set B.

SET A: Set A starts with a black shape. A line then takes us to a white shape. A line then takes us to a grey shape. A line then takes us to a black shape.

SET B: Set B starts with a black shape. A line then takes us to a grey shape. A line then takes us to a black shape. A line then takes us to a black shape.

Q13. NEITHER

The Test Shape doesn't fit in to either Sets. The Test Shape follows the colour pattern of black, white, black and grey. In Set A, the colour pattern goes black, white, grey and black and Set B goes black, grey, black and black, so therefore cannot fit into either sequence.

SET A: Set A starts with a black shape. A line then takes us to a white shape. A line then takes us to a grey shape. A line then takes us to a black shape.

SET B: Set B starts with a black shape. A line then takes us to a grey shape. A line then takes us to a black shape. A line then takes us to a black shape.

Q14. SET A

The Test Shape fits in to Set A. The Test Shape starts with a white shape, it is linked to two shapes. It links a white shape to a black shape. The line leading from the white shape leads to a grey shape. The line leading from the black shape leads to a white shape. This follows the same pattern as Set A.

SET A: Set A starts with a white shape. A vertical line then takes us to horizontal line with 2 shapes at each end. To the left is a white shape and to the right is a black shape. The line leading from the white shape takes us to a grey shape. The line leading from the black shape takes us to a white shape.

SET B: Set B starts with a white shape. A vertical line then takes us to horizontal line with 2 shapes at each end. To the left is a white shape and to the right is a black shape. The line leading from the white shape takes us to another white shape. The line leading from the black shape takes us to a grey shape.

Q15. TEST SHAPE C

The sequence of Set A starts with a white shape. It then links a black shape to a black shape. The line leading from the first black shape leads to a grey shape. The line leading from the second black shape leads to a white shape. Therefore, only Test Shape C fits in with this sequence.

SET A: Set A starts with a white shape. A vertical line then takes us to horizontal line with 2 shapes at each end. To the left is a black shape and to the right is a black shape also. The line leading from the left black shape takes us to a grey shape. The line leading from the right black shape takes us to a white shape.

Q16. NEITHER

Neither of the Test Shapes fit in with Set B. Set B's pattern goes from a white shape and links it to another white shape and a grey shape. The line leading from the white shape goes to another white shape. The line leading from the grey shape goes to another grey shape. None of the Test Shapes follow this pattern.

SET B: Set B starts with a white shape. A vertical line then takes us to horizontal line with 2 shapes at each end. To the left is a white shape and to the right is a grey shape. The line leading from the white shape takes us to another white shape. The line leading from the grey shape takes us to another grey shape.

Q17. NEITHER

Neither of the Test Shapes fit in with Set A. Set A's sequence starts with a grey shape, it then links a black shape to another black shape. The line leading from the first black shape links to a white shape. The line leading from the second black shape also leads to a white shape. None of the Test Shapes follow this pattern.

SET A: Set A starts with a grey shape. A vertical line then takes us to horizontal line with 2 black shapes at each end. Each black shape leads to a white shape.

Q18. TEST SHAPE A

The sequence to Set B starts with a black shape, it then links a white shape to a black shape. The line leading from the white shape goes to a grey shape. The line leading from the black shape goes to a grey shape. Only Test Shape A follows this pattern.

SET B: Set B starts with a white shape. A vertical line then takes us to horizontal line with 2 shapes at each end. To the left is a white shape and to the right is a black shape. Each shape then leads to a grey shape.

Q19. TEST SHAPE B

The sequence to Set A begins with a grey shape, it then leads to a black shape and a grey shape, under these shapes follows the colour patter black, black, white and white. Only Test Shape B follows this pattern.

SET A: Set A starts with a grey shape. A vertical line then takes us to horizontal line with 2 shapes at each end. To the left is a black shape and to the right is a grey shape. The line leading from the left black shape takes us to another black shape. The line leading from the right grey shape takes us to a white shape.

Q20. TEST SHAPE A

The sequence of Set B starts with a black shape. It then links a white shape to a black shape. The shapes underneath follow the pattern black, white, black and grey. Only Test Shape A follows this pattern.

SET B: Set B starts with a black shape. A vertical line then takes us to horizontal line with 2 shapes at each end. To the left is a white shape and to the right is a black shape. The line leading from the white shape takes us to a black shape. The line leading from the black shape takes us to a grey shape. There are also 2 central lines leading down to two circular shapes. The circular shape to the left is white and the one to the right is black.

ABSTRACT REASONING TEST
SECTION 2

*In abstract reasoning test section 2 there are 20 questions
and you have just 10 minutes to answer them*

ABSTRACT REASONING TEST SECTION 2

Q1. Which figure completes the series?

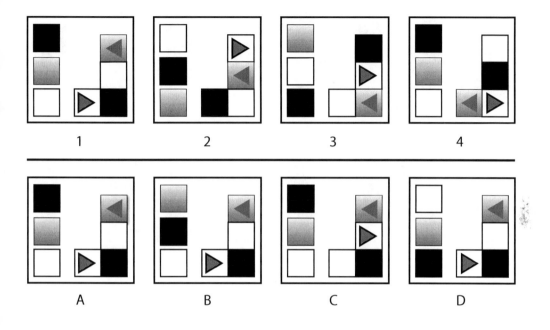

1   2   3   4

A   B   C   D

A   ◯

B   ◯

C   ◯

D   ◯

NEITHER   ◯

Q2. Which figure completes the series?

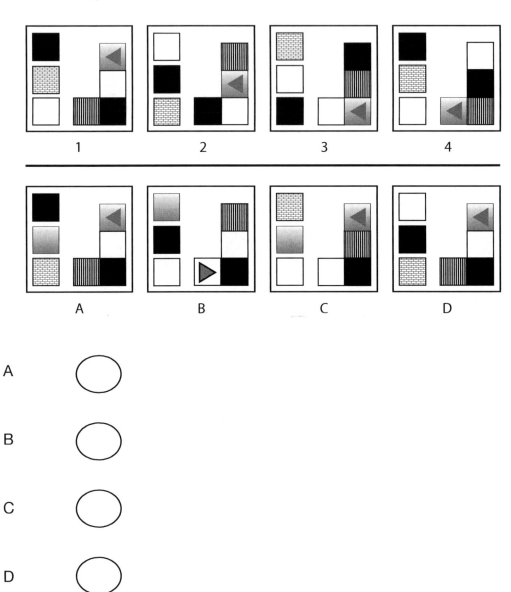

A ○

B ○

C ○

D ○

NEITHER ○

Q3. Which figure completes the series?

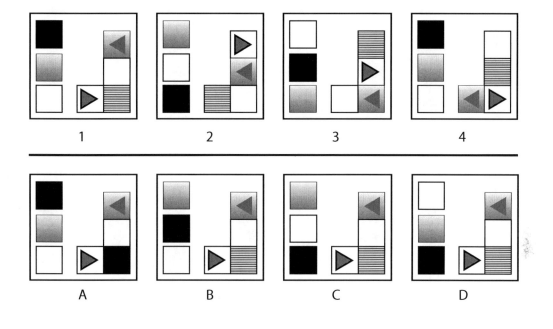

A ◯

B ◯

C ◯

D ◯

NEITHER ◯

Q4. Which figure completes the series?

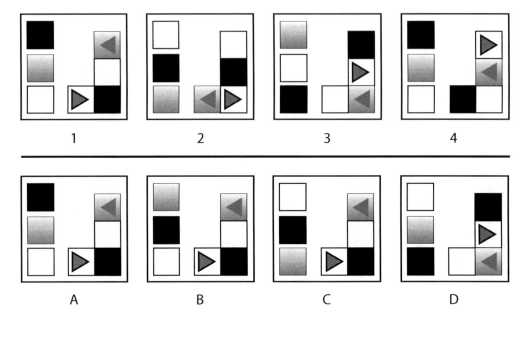

A ◯

B ◯

C ◯

D ◯

NEITHER ◯

Q5. Which figure completes the series?

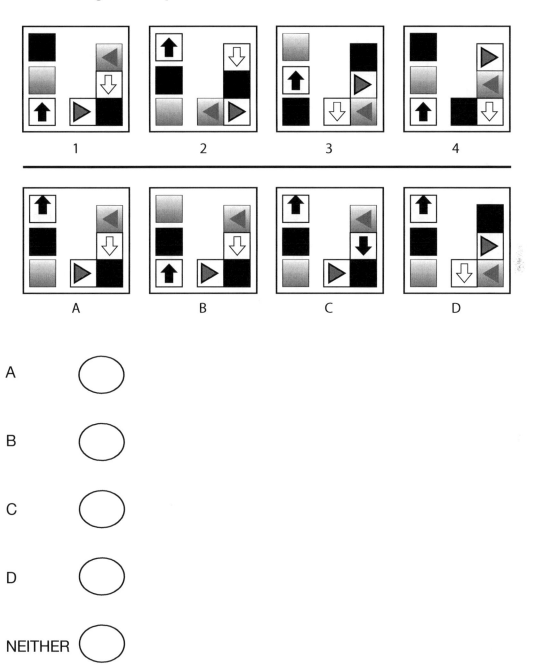

A ◯

B ◯

C ◯

D ◯

NEITHER ◯

Q6. Which figure completes the series?

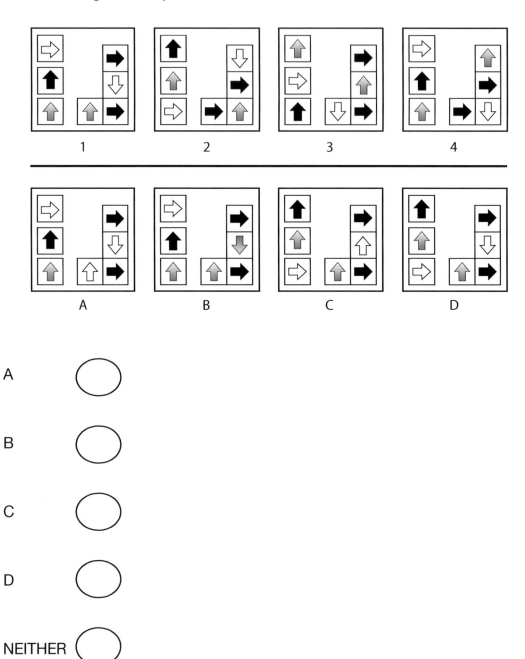

A ◯

B ◯

C ◯

D ◯

NEITHER ◯

Q7. Which figure completes the series?

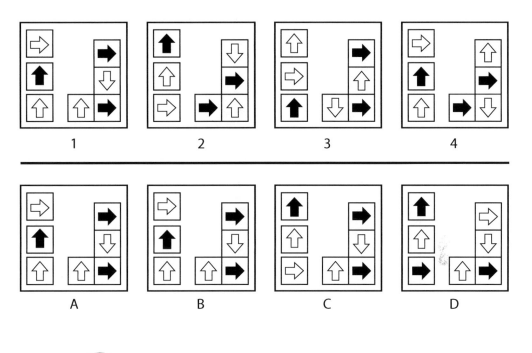

1   2   3   4

A   B   C   D

A

B

C

D   ◯

NEITHER

Q8. Which figure completes the series?

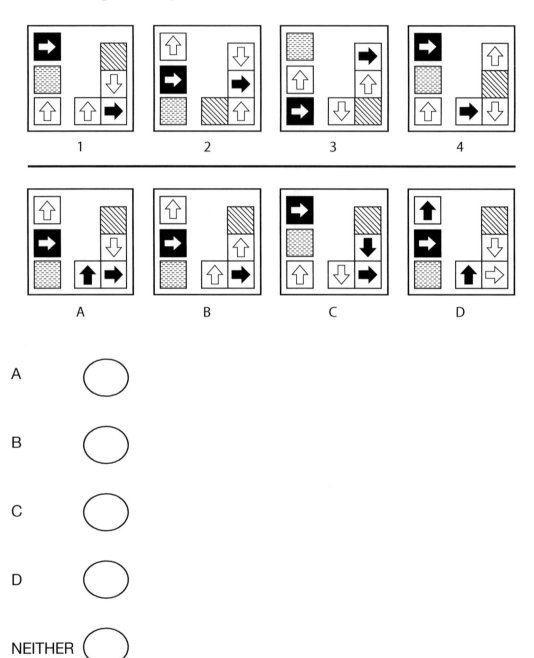

A ○

B ○

C ○

D ○

NEITHER ○

Q9. Which figure comes next in the series?

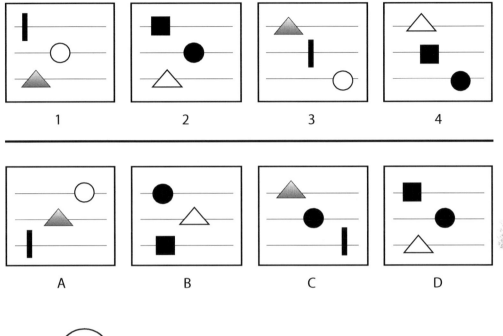

1   2   3   4

A   B   C   D

A   ◯

B   ◯

C   ◯

D   ◯

NEITHER   ◯

Q10. Which figure comes next in the series?

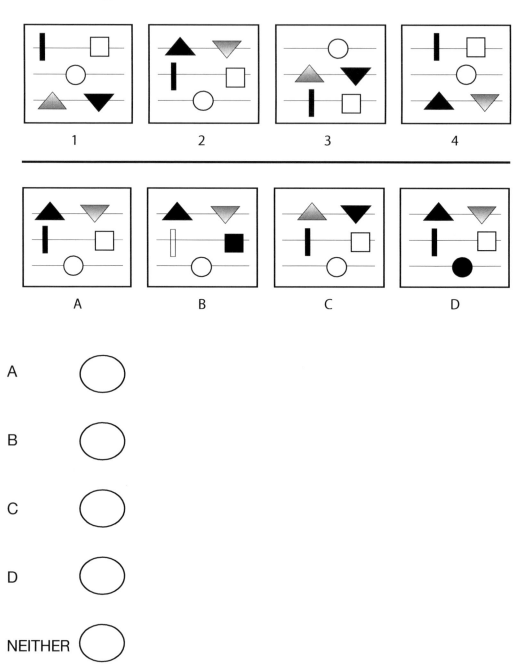

A ◯

B ◯

C ◯

D ◯

NEITHER ◯

Q11. Which figure comes next in the series?

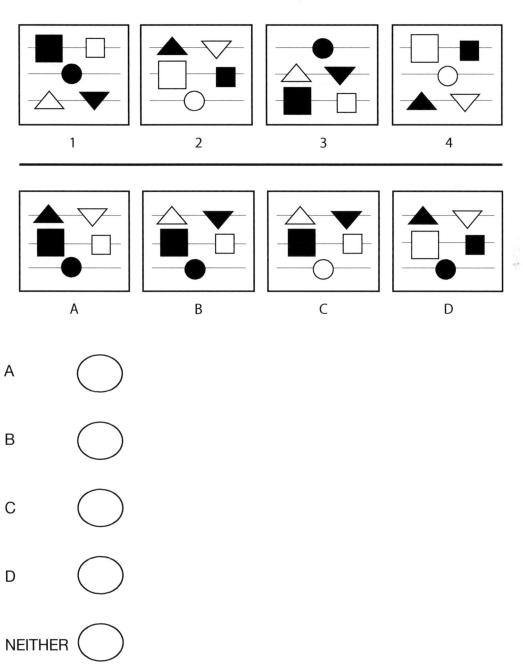

A ◯

B ◯

C ◯

D ◯

NEITHER ◯

Q12. Which figure comes next in the series?

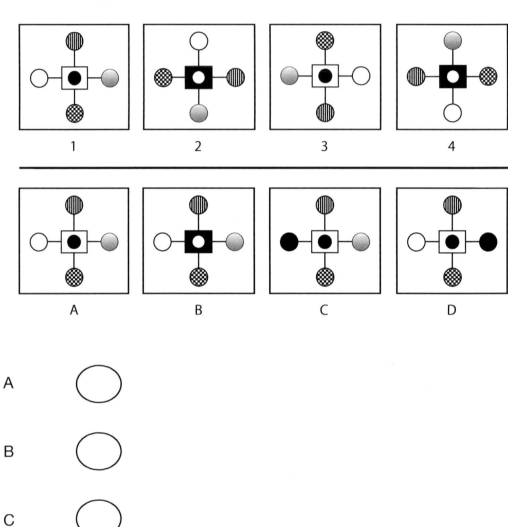

A ◯

B ◯

C ◯

D ◯

NEITHER ◯

Q13. Which figure comes next in the series?

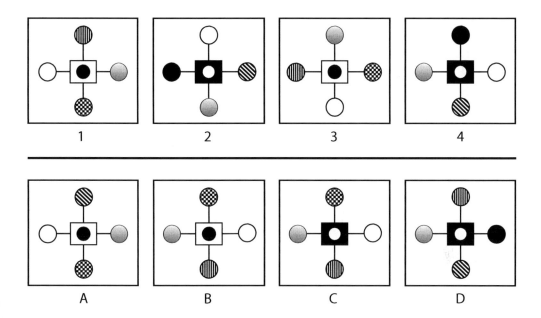

A

B   ◯

C   ◯

D   ◯

NEITHER   ◯

Q14. Which figure comes next in the series?

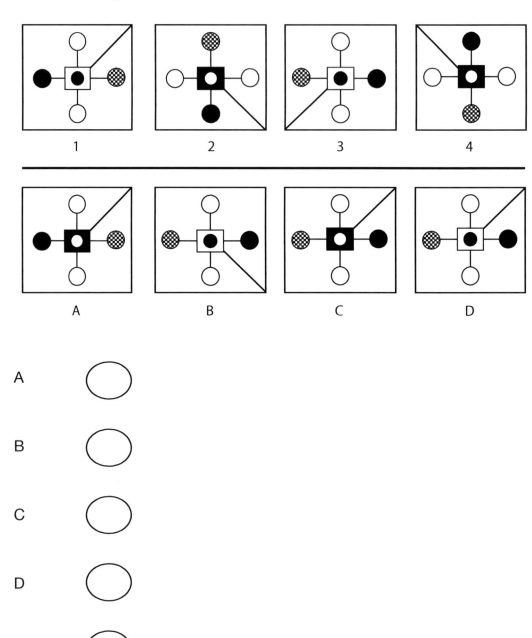

1   2   3   4

A   B   C   D

A ○

B ○

C ○

D ○

NEITHER ○

15. Which figure comes next in the series?

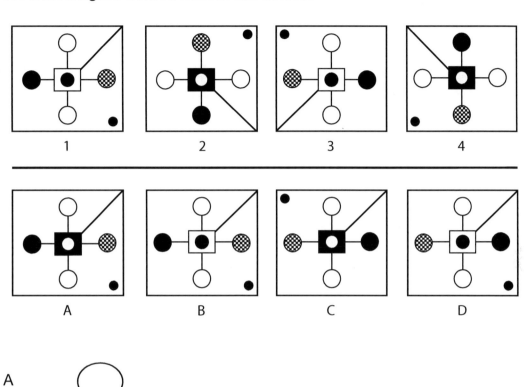

1   2   3   4

A   B   C   D

A ◯

B ◯

C ◯

D ◯

NEITHER ◯

Q16. Which figure comes next in the series?

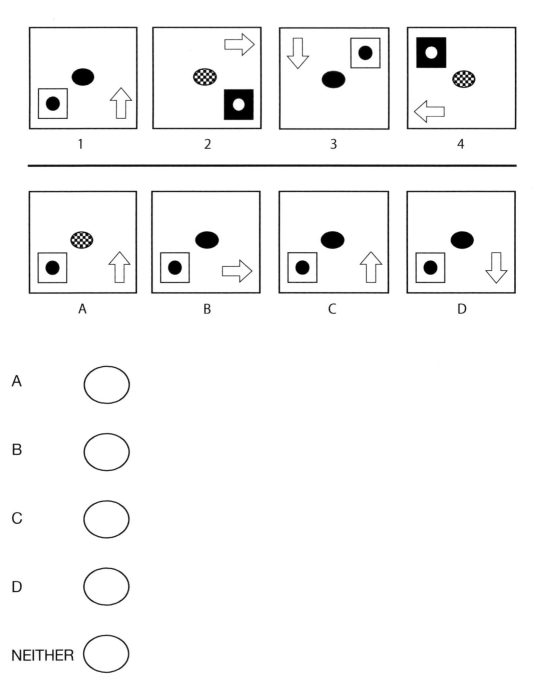

A ◯

B ◯

C ◯

D ◯

NEITHER ◯

Q17. Which figure comes next in the series?

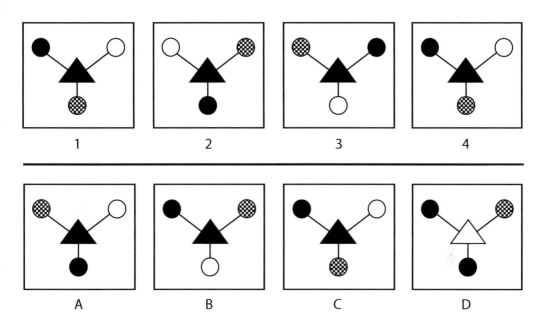

A ○

B ○

C ○

D ○

NEITHER ○

Q18. Which figure comes next in the series?

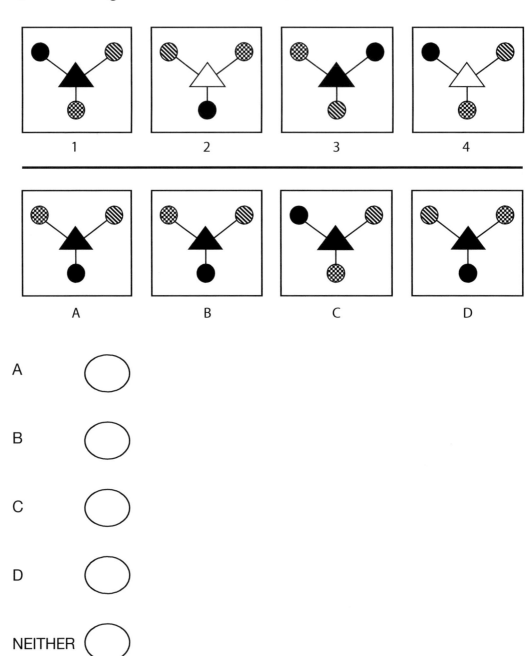

A ◯

B ◯

C ◯

D ◯

NEITHER ◯

Q19. Which figure comes next in the series?

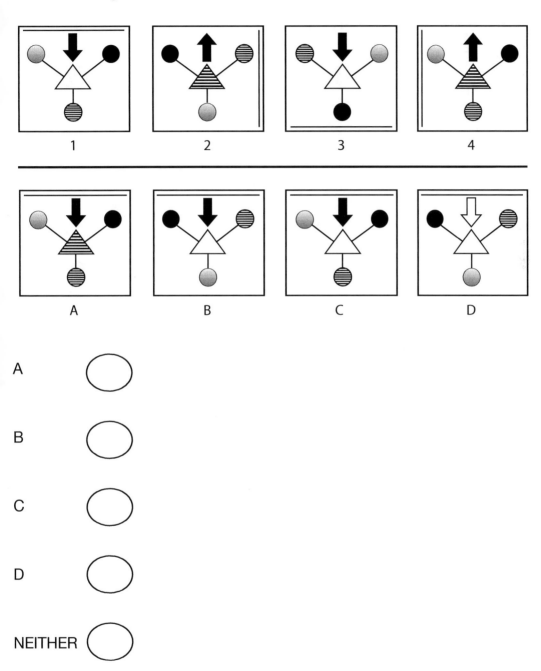

1

2

3

4

A

B

C

D

A ◯

B ◯

C ◯

D ◯

NEITHER ◯

Q20. Which figure comes next in the series?

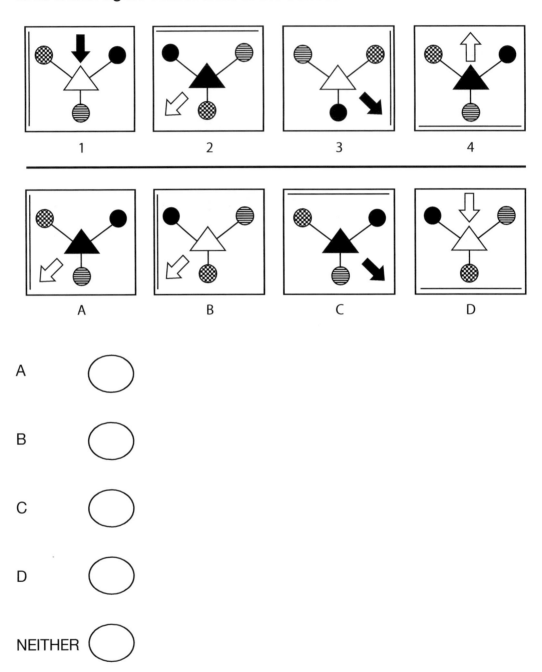

A ⬭

B ⬭

C ⬭

D ⬭

NEITHER ⬭

Please now check your answers carefully before moving on to the next section of the guide.

ANSWERS TO ABSTRACT REASONING TEST SECTION 2

Q1. B

Within each square of the series, the 3 squares to the left move down one as the sequence progresses.

Within each square of the series, the 4 shapes to the right move down one as the sequence progresses.

Q2. D

Within each square of the series, the 3 squares to the left move down one as the sequence progresses.

Within each square of the series, the 4 shapes to the right move down one as the sequence progresses.

Q3. C

Within each square of the series, the 3 squares to the left move up one as the sequence progresses.

Within each square of the series, the 4 shapes to the right move down one as the sequence progresses.

Q4. C

Within each square of the series, the 3 squares to the left move down one as the sequence progresses.

Within each square of the series, the 4 shapes to the right move up one as the sequence progresses.

Q5. A

Within each square of the series, the 3 squares to the left move down one as the sequence progresses.

Within each square of the series, the 4 shapes to the right move up one as the sequence progresses.

Q6. D

Within each square of the series, the 3 squares to the left move up one as the sequence progresses.

Within each square of the series, the 4 shapes to the right move up one as the sequence progresses.

Q7. C

Within each square of the series, the 3 squares to the left move up one as the sequence progresses.

Within each square of the series, the 4 shapes to the right move up one as the sequence progresses.

Q8. NEITHER

Within each square of the series, the 3 squares to the left move down one as the sequence progresses.

Within each square of the series, the 4 shapes to the right move up one as the sequence progresses.

Q9. A

Within each odd square (square 1 and 3), the shapes are moving down each line as the sequence progresses.

Within the even squares (square 2 and 4), the shapes are moving down each line as the sequence progresses.

Q10. C

Within each square the shapes are moving down each line as the sequence progresses. Once they reach the bottom they go back to the top. However, you will notice that the two triangular shapes alternate colours, switching from black to grey and vice versa, as the sequence progresses.

Q11. B

Within each square the shapes are moving down each line as the sequence progresses. Once they reach the bottom they go back to the top. However, you will notice that each set of shapes alternate colours, switching from black to white and vice versa, as the sequence progresses.

Q12. A

Within each square the shapes are moving round clockwise as the sequence progresses. You will also notice that the square and inner circle which form the centre of each shape are alternating between black and white as the sequence progresses.

Q13. B

Within each odd numbered square (1 and 3) the shapes are moving round anti-clockwise as the sequence progresses whilst the central square and circle stay the same colours respectively. Within each even numbered square (2 and 4) the shapes are moving round clockwise as the sequence progresses whilst the central square and circle stay the same colours respectively.

Q14. NEITHER

Within each square the shapes are moving round anti-clockwise as the sequence progresses. You will also notice that the square and inner circle which form the centre of each shape are each alternating between black and white as the sequence progresses. The diagonal line within each square is moving round clockwise as the sequence progresses.

Q15. B

Within each square the shapes are moving round clockwise as the sequence progresses. You will also notice that the square and inner circle which form the centre of each shape are each alternating between black and white as the sequence progresses. The diagonal line within each square is moving round clockwise as the sequence progresses. The small black dot in the corner of each square is moving round anti-clockwise as the sequence progresses.

Q16. C

Within each square the shapes are all moving round in an anti-clockwise manner as the sequence progresses. The inner circle is alternating between black and chequered as the sequence progresses. The square and small inner circle are alternating between black and white as the sequence progresses. The arrow within each square is spinning clockwise as the sequence progresses.

Q17. NEITHER

Within each square the circles are all moving round in an anti-clockwise manner as the sequence progresses.

Q18. D

Within each square the circles are all moving round in an anti-clockwise manner as the sequence progresses.

Q19. B

Within each square the circles are all moving round in an anti-clockwise manner as the sequence progresses. The straight line which is parallel to one side of the square is moving round in a clockwise manner as the sequence progresses. The central triangle is alternating between white and stripes as the sequence progresses. The black arrow at the top of the triangle is alternating between pointing upwards and downwards as the sequence progresses.

Q20. NEITHER

Within each square the circles are all moving round in an anti-clockwise manner as the sequence progresses. The straight line which is parallel to one side of the square is moving round in a clockwise manner as the sequence progresses. The central triangle is alternating between white and black as the sequence progresses. The arrow moving around the triangle in an anti-clockwise manner and is alternating between black and white as the sequence progresses.

ABSTRACT REASONING TEST
SECTION 3

In abstract reasoning test section 3 there are 20 questions and you have just 10 minutes to answer them

ABSTRACT REASONING TEST SECTION 3

Question 1

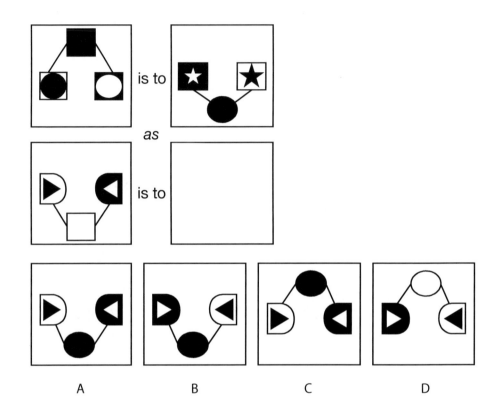

A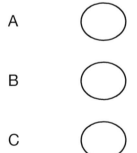

B ◯

C ◯

D ◯

NEITHER

Question 2

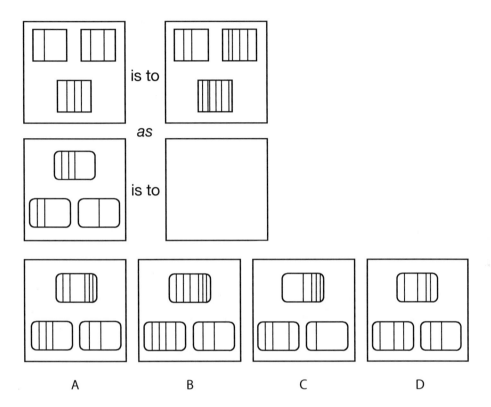

A

B

C

D

NEITHER

Question 3

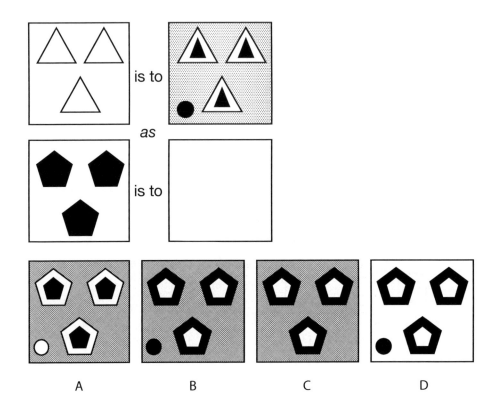

A

B

C

D

NEITHER

Question 4

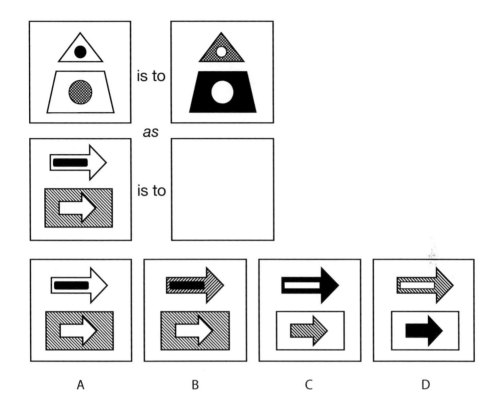

is to

as

is to

A   B   C   D

A

B ◯

C ◯

D ◯

NEITHER ◯

Question 5

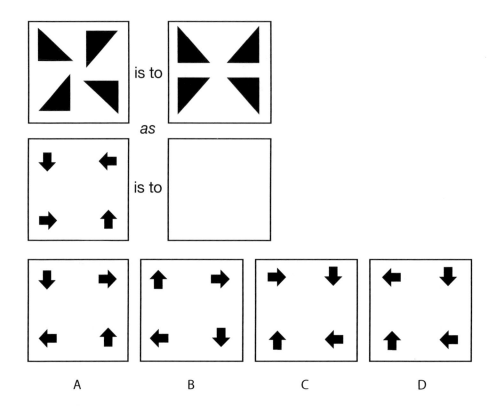

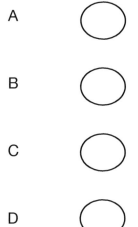

Question 6

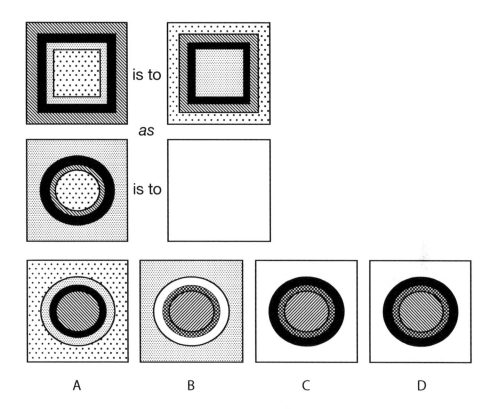

A ◯

B ◯

C ◯

D ◯

NEITHER ◯

Question 7

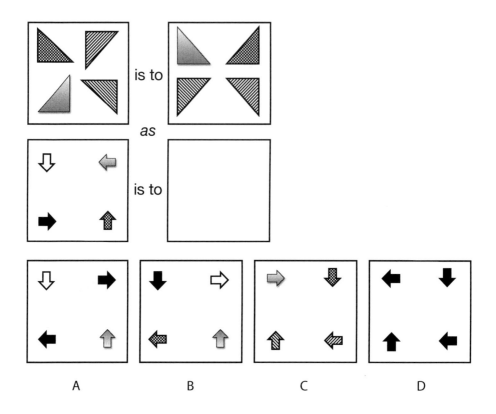

A

○

B

○

C

○

D

○

NEITHER ○

Question 8

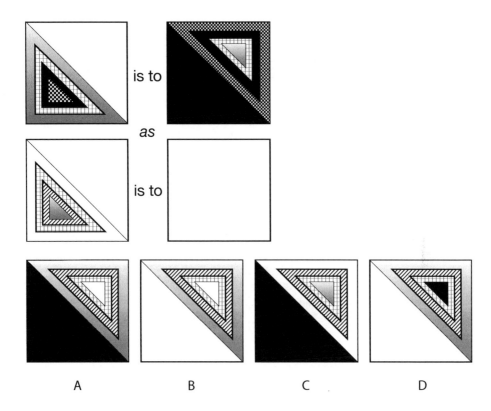

is to

as

is to

A	B	C	D

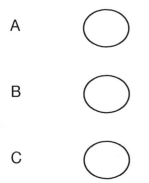

A ◯

B ◯

C ◯

D ◯

NEITHER ◯

Question 9

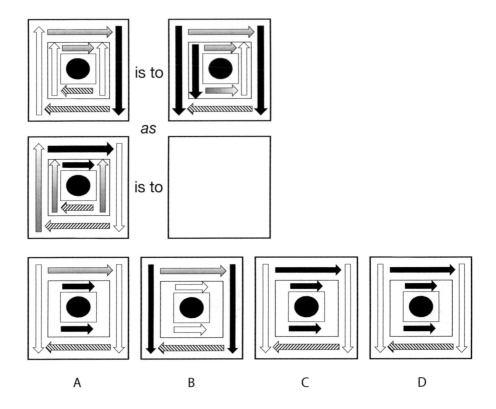

A

○

B

○

C

○

D

○

NEITHER ○

Question 10

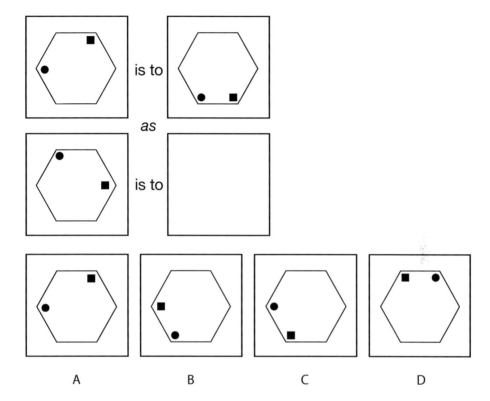

A

B

C

D

NEITHER

Question 11

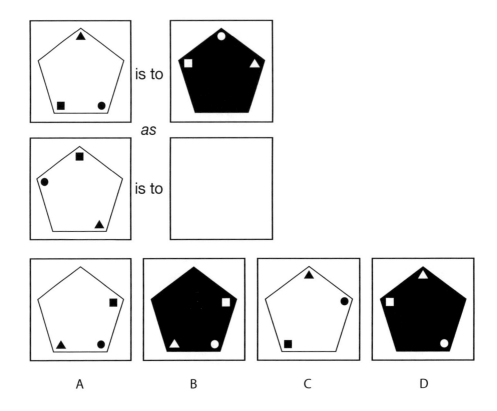

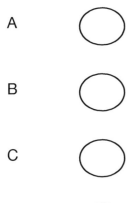

Question 12

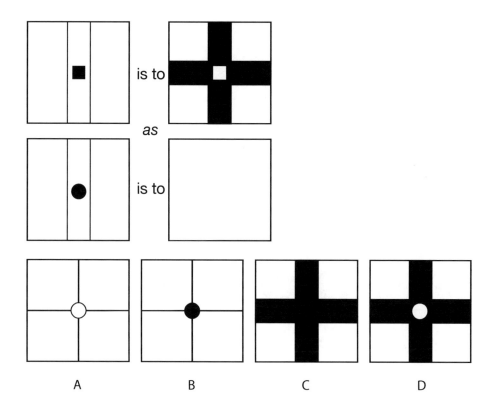

A

B

C

D

NEITHER

Question 13

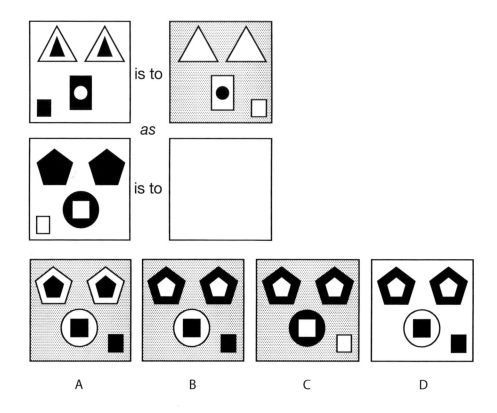

A   B   C   D

A   ◯

B   ◯

C   ◯

D   ◯

NEITHER   ◯

Question 14

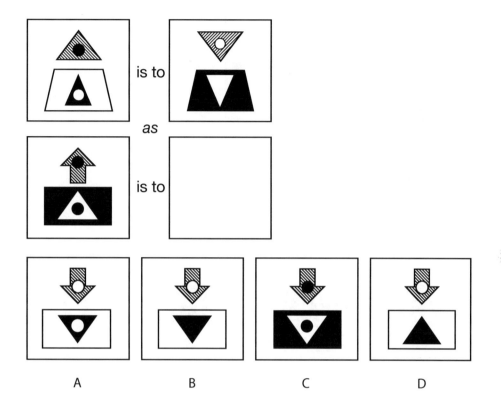

A   B   C   D

A   ⚪

B   ⚪

C   ⚪

D   ⚪

NEITHER   ⚪

Question 15

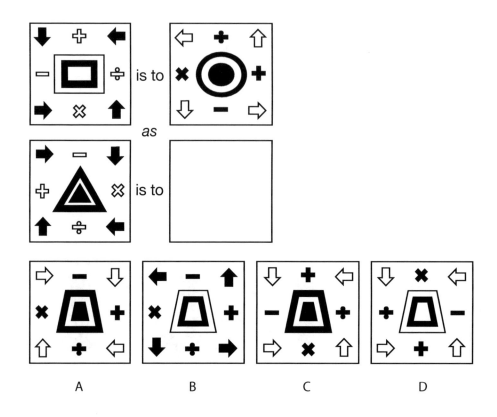

A

B

C

D

NEITHER

Question 16

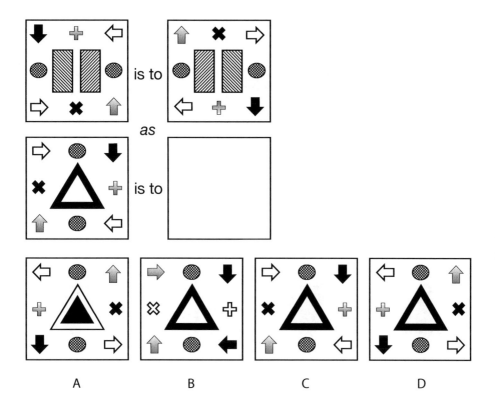

A ◯

B ◯

C ◯

D ◯

NEITHER ◯

Question 17

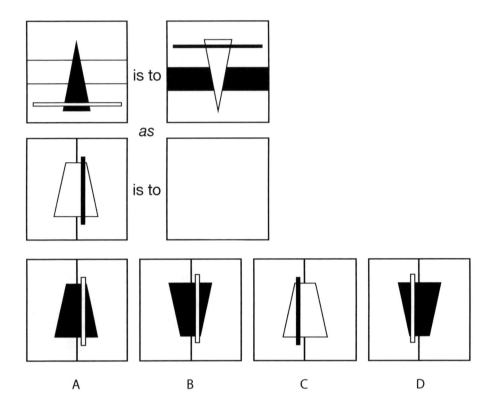

A ◯

B ◯

C ◯

D ◯

NEITHER ◯

Question 18

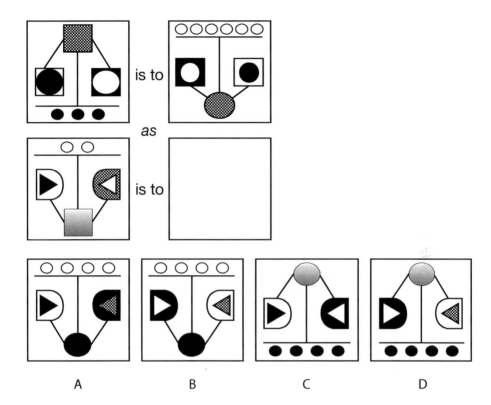

A   B   C   D

A

B ◯

C ◯

D ◯

NEITHER ◯

Question 19

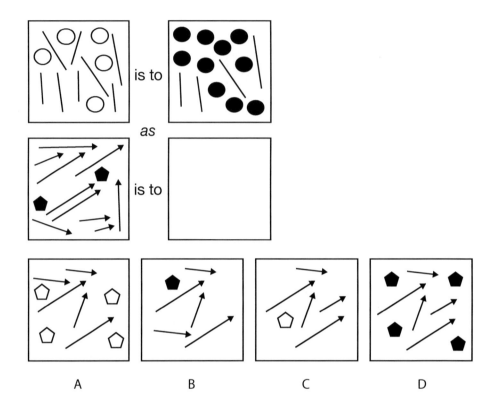

A

B

C

D

NEITHER

Question 20

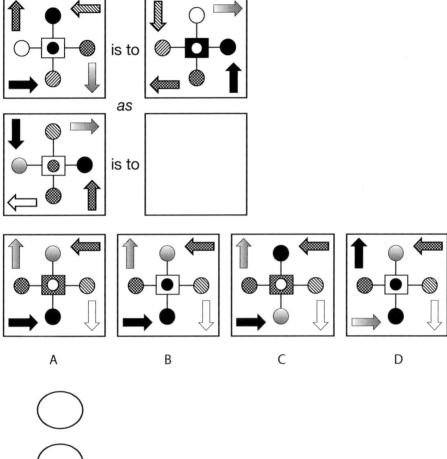

A   B   C   D

A ◯

B ◯

C ◯

D ◯

NEITHER ◯

Please now check your answers carefully before moving on to the next section of your guide.

ANSWERS TO ABSTRACT REASONING TEST SECTION 3

Q1. D

To reach the answer, the bottom shape needs to be flipped horizontally and the colours inverted.

Within the first set of squares the shapes in the second square are turned upside down. The top black square within the first square is replaced with a black circle in the second and the two squares with internal shapes near the centre alternate between black and white.

Therefore, the bottom set of squares will need to follow the same format. Option D the correct answer and replaces the white square at the bottom with a white circle near the top. The two shapes near the centre of Option D with internal triangles alternate between black and white.

Q2. B

Within the first set of shapes the corresponding lines within each square are doubling each time.

Q3. B

Within the first (top) set of shapes there are additional smaller triangles of an alternate colour within the larger triangles. There is also a black dot in the bottom left hand corner of the main square and the background is shaded. Therefore, to reach the answer the pentagons must have smaller pentagons of an inverted colour, shaded background and a black dot. This makes the correct answer B.

Q4. D

Within the first set of shapes the colours and chequered shading alternate between the top and lower shapes. For example, the white triangle with the black circle at the top within the first square becomes a black rectangle with a white circle at the bottom of the second square.

Q5. A

Within the top set of squares the top left and bottom right shapes remain in the same position. The bottom left and top right shapes rotate 180 degrees.

Q6. A

Within the top left-hand square the different coloured/shaded squares work from the outside towards the centre. Within the top right-hand square the different coloured/shaded squares work from the centre towards the outside.

Q7. B

Within the top set of squares the top left and bottom right shapes remain in the same position. The bottom left and top right shapes each rotate through 180 degrees. Within the top right square the colours and shades each move round one place clockwise

Q8. A

Within the top left hand square the pattern of triangular shapes is in the bottom left corner of the square, with the patterns and shades starting on the outside and working in towards the centre. Within the top right hand square the pattern of triangular shapes is in the top right corner of the square, only this time the patterns and shades work from the centre to the outside.

Q9. C

Within the top two sqaures the arrows pointing to the right are grey, arrows pointing to the left have diagonal stripes pointing from top left to bottom right, arrows pointing down are black and arrows pointing up are white. Within the bottom two sqaures the arrows pointing to the right are black, arrows pointing to the left have diagonal stripes from bottom left to top right, arrows pointing down are white and arrows pointing up are grey.

Q10. C

In the top set of squares the small black circle moves around the hexagon anti-clockwise one place. The small black square moves around the hexagon clockwise two places.

Q11. B

In the top set of squares the left hand side hexagon is white with black shapes whereas the right hand side hexagon is black with white shapes. The small black circle moves around the hexagon anti-clockwise two places. The small black square moves around the hexagon clockwise one place. The small black triangle clockwise one place.

Q12. D

In the top left square there is a vertical white rectangle running through the centre with a black square. In the top right square the shape changes to a black cross and white square.

Q13. B

In the top left square there are two white triangles, each with smaller black triangles inside. There is also a black rectangle with an inner white circle. The background to the main square is white with a black rectangle in the bottom left corner. In the top right square the two white triangles lose their inner black triangles. The larger rectangle and inner circle change colour from black to white and vice versa. The background to the main square is now shaded and the small rectangle switches sides and is now on the right and is also white.

Q14. B

In the top left square there is a striped triangle with a black circle in the centre. Below this is a white trapezium with black triangle with a white circle. In the top right hand square the striped triangle is now inverted and the circle is black. Below this the trapezium is now black, the inner triangle inverted and white with no central circle.

Q15. D

In the top set of squares the arrows are moving around the square anticlockwise one place each time and changing from black to white. The mathematical symbols are moving around the square clockwise one place each time and are changing from white to black. The central rectangular shapes become circular and each section changes from black to white and vice versa.

Q16. A

In the top set of squares the each shape is either the same colour, shade or pattern. For example, arrows pointing down and the multiplication symbols are black, arrows pointing either left or right are white and circles are chequered etc. The only difference between the items in the left square and the right square are that each symbol swaps sides or corner. In the first square, the black arrow pointing downwards in the top left hand corner is now in the bottom right hand corner of the right square etc.

Q17. D

In the top set of squares the rectangle changes from white to black. The triangle changes from black to white and becomes inverted. The thin rectangle goes from white and being in the bottom half to being black and being in the top half.

Q18. D

Within the first set of squares the shapes in the second square are turned upside down. The top chequered square within the first square is replaced with a chequered circle in the second, and the two squares with internal shapes near the centre alternate between black and white. The number of circles doubles and changes from black to white in the second square.

Q19. A

Within the first set of squares the circles double in number from 5 to 10 and change from white to black. The number of straight lines halves from 8 to 4.

Q20. A

In the top set of squares the colours and shading of the outer arrows are moving around the square anti-clockwise one place each time. The arrows are also rotating 180 degrees. The colours and shading of the circles are moving around the central axis clockwise one place each time. The central rectangle and inner circle change from white to black and vice versa.

ABSTRACT REASONING TEST
SECTION 4

In abstract reasoning test section 4 there are 20 questions and you have just 10 minutes to answer them

ABSTRACT REASONING TEST SECTION 4

Q1. Which figure comes next in the sequence?

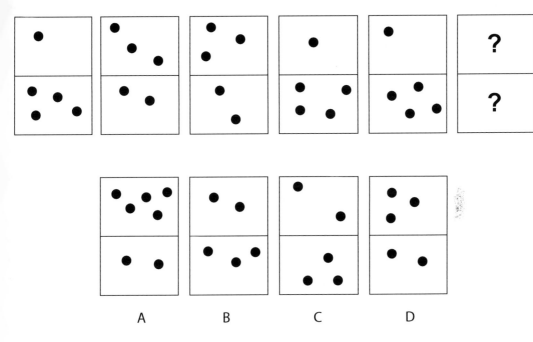

A B C D

A ◯

B ◯

C ◯

D ◯

Q2. Which figure comes next in the sequence?

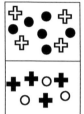 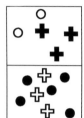 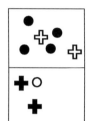 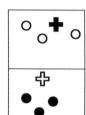 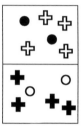 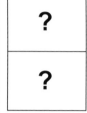

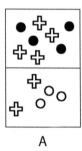 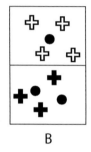 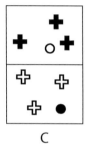 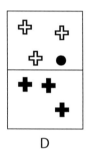

A   B   C   D

A

B

C ◯

D

Q3. Which figure comes next in the sequence?

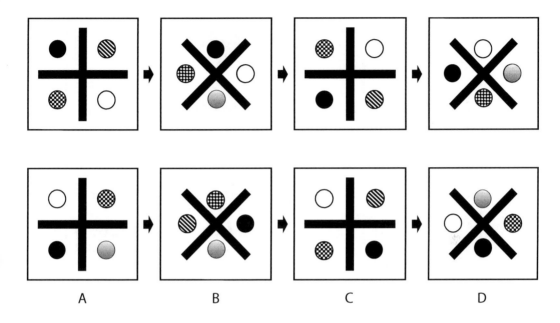

A	B	C	D

A ⬭

B ⬭

C ⬭

D ⬭

Q4. Which figure comes next in the sequence?

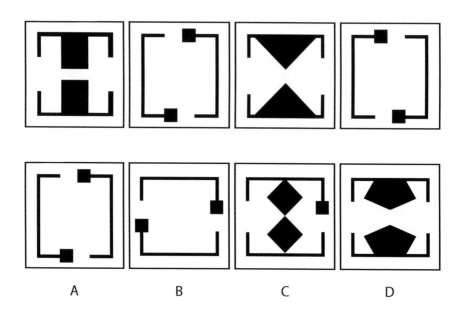

A

B

C

D

A ◯

B ◯

C ◯

D ◯

Q5. Which figure is the odd one out?

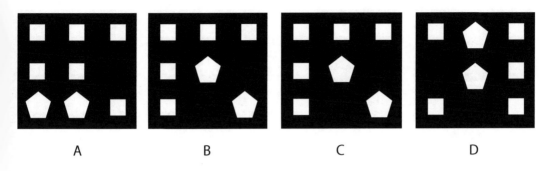

A   B   C   D

A ◯

B ◯

C ◯

D ◯

Q6. Which figure is the odd one out?

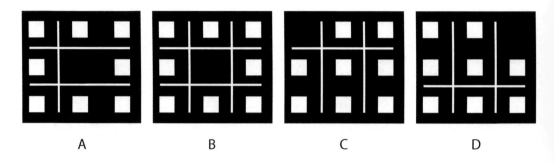

A   B   C   D

A ◯

B ◯

C ◯

D ◯

Q7. Which figure is the odd one out?

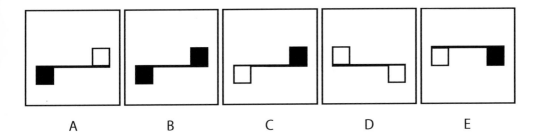

A   B   C   D   E

A   ◯

B   ◯

C   ◯

D   ◯

Q8. Which figure comes next in the sequence?

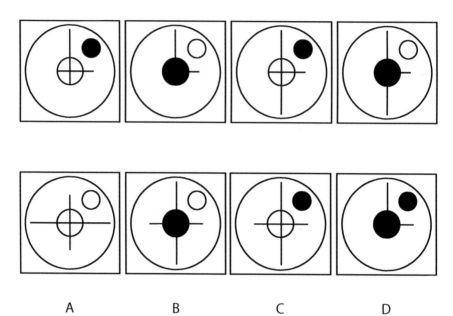

A   B   C   D

A ◯

B ◯

C ◯

D ◯

Q9. Which figure comes next in the sequence?

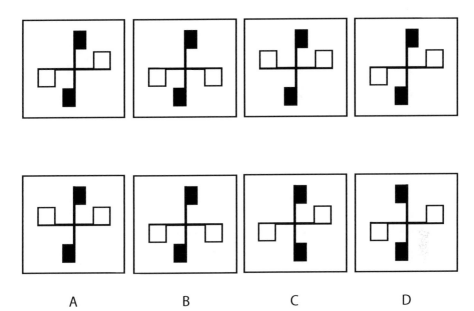

A   B   C   D

A

B

C

D

Q10. Which figure comes next in the sequence?

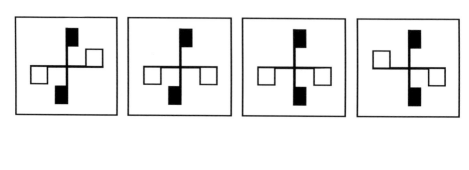

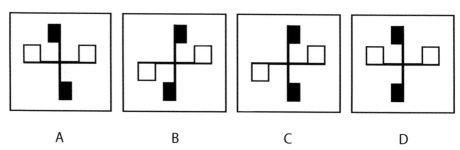

A   B   C   D

A   ◯

B   ◯

C   ◯

D   ◯

Q11. Which figure comes next in the sequence?

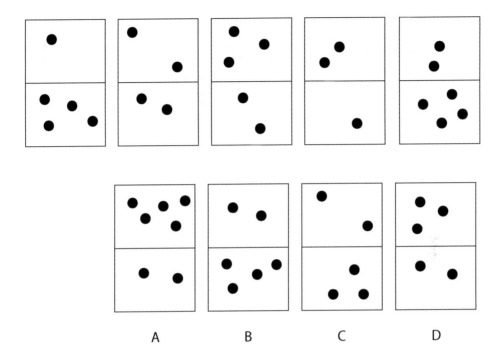

A

B

C

D

A ⬭

B ⬭

C ⬭

D ⬭

Q12. Which figure is the odd one out?

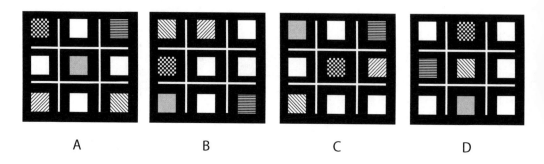

A   B   C   D

A ◯

B ◯

C ◯

D ◯

Q13. Which figure is the odd one out?

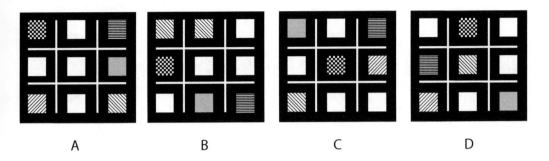

A   B   C   D

A ◯

B ◯

C ◯

D ◯

Q14. Which figure comes next in the sequence?

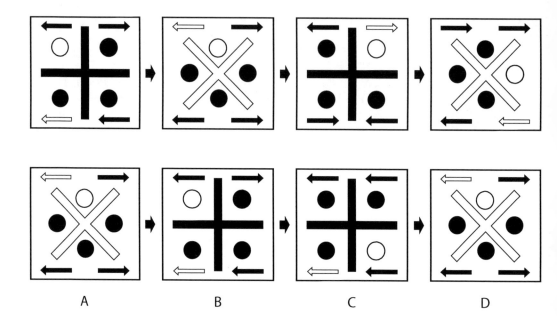

A   B   C   D

A ◯

B ◯

C ◯

D ◯

Q15. Which figure comes next in the sequence?

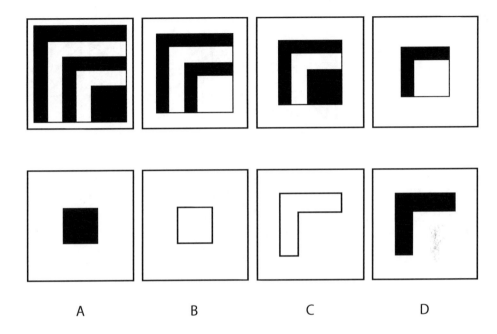

A   B   C   D

A ◯

B ◯

C ◯

D ◯

Q16. Which figure comes next in the sequence?

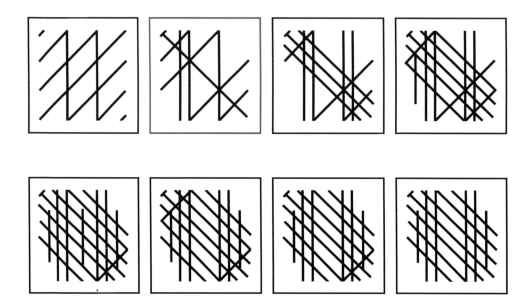

A   B   C   D

A ◯

B ◯

C ◯

D ◯

Q17. Which figure comes next in the sequence?

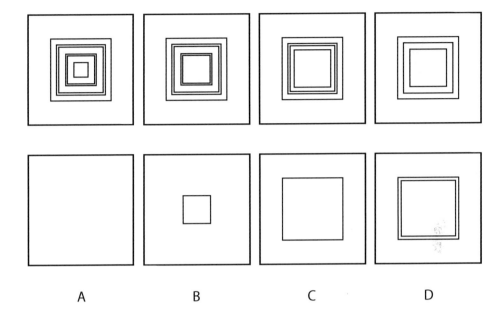

A   B   C   D

A

B ◯

C ◯

D ◯

Q18. Which figure comes next in the sequence?

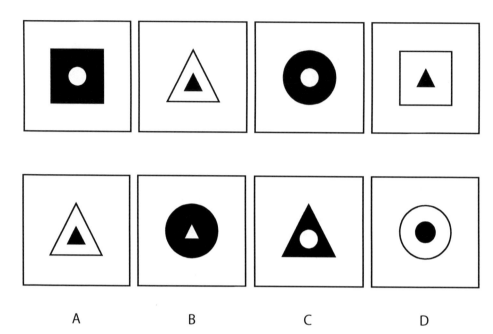

A

B

C

D

A ⬭

B ⬭

C ⬭

D ⬭

Q19. Which figure comes next in the sequence?

A   B   C   D

A

B

C ⬭

D

Q20. Which figure comes next in the sequence?

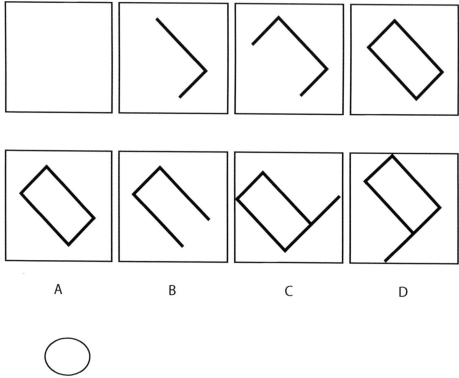

A   B   C   D

A   ◯

B   ◯

C   ◯

D   ◯

Please now check your answers carefully.

ANSWERS TO ABSTRACT REASONING TEST SECTION 4

Q1. D

The number of dots starts off as 1 in top of the first rectangle and 4 in the bottom. As the sequence progresses the number of dots either increases or decreases in the alternate section of the rectangle until it reaches 4, when the sequence starts again.

Q2. C

The number of dots starts off as 6 black ones in top of the first rectangle and 3 white ones in the bottom. The number of plus signs starts of as 4 white ones in the top rectangle and 4 black ones in the bottom. As the sequence progresses the number of dots and plus signs decreases in the alternate section of the rectangle until it reaches 1, when the sequence starts again.

Q3. C

The sequence alternates between a plus sign and a cross sign, each with circular shapes moving around the signs in an anti-clockwise manner. Therefore, the correct answer is C.

Q4. D

The sequence alternates between solid black shapes inside horizontal 'brackets' and vertical brackets with a black square at one end of each bracket. Therefore, the correct answer is D as this is the only option that is similar to shapes 1 and 3 in the sequence.

Q5. A

Figure A is the only one with 6 white squares. All of the other figures have 5.

Q6. B

Figure B is the only one with 4 white lines and 8 white squares. All of the other figures have 3 white lines and 8 squares.

Q7. E

Figure E is the only one without either a black or white square on the upper-most portion of the horizontal black line.

Q8. C

The figures in the sequence are alternating between white/black circles and vice versa. The vertical and horizontal lines are also increasing by 1 each time within each odd and even numbered figure.

Q9. B

Answer B is reached because the two white squares move in the following 3-piece sequence: 1 up and 1 down, both down, both up, 1 up and 1 down, both down etc.

Q10. A

Throughout the duration of the sequence each 'attached' shape switches sides once during the sequence and then stays in that position for the remainder of the sequence. Once the attached shape switches sides in the sequence the next attached shape in the clockwise position switches sides.

Q11. C

Starting from the top left in the first rectangle the number of dots is 1, this then works in a zig-zag patteren through to rectangle 5 of 1,2,3,1,2,3 etc. The bottom left works similar with the patteren of 4,22,4,4,22,4 etc.

Q12. D

Figure D is the only one with 5 white squares. All of the other figures have 4 white squares and the same number and type of alternative shades and patterns.

Q13. B

Figure B is the only one with 2 white squares with diagonal lines the same. All of the other figures have 2 white squares with diagonal lines but in the opposite direction/angle.

Q14. C

The sequence alternates between a plus sign and a cross sign, each with 3 black circular shapes and 1 white circular shapes located around the signs. Each figure also has 3 black arrows and 1 white arrow located around the inner edge of the outer square. As the sequence progresses the white circular shape in each figure moves around its own shape 1 position in a clockwise manner. In addition to this, one of the arrows around the outer edge goes from black to white and vice versa in a clockwise manner. In addition, one of the arrows changes direction as the sequence progresses before reverting back to its original position in the next figure.

Q15. A

Each figure is losing one element at a time as the sequence progresses and the square alternates from black to white.

Q16. C

The vertical lines are increasing by one each time as the sequence progresses: 2, 3, 4, 5, 6 etc. The diagonal lines which run from top left to bottom right are increasing at odd numbers each time as the sequence progresses: 0, 1, 3, 5, 7 etc.

Q17. D

Each figure is losing one square working from the centre outwards as the sequence progresses.

Q18. C

The outer shape sequence goes: Square, triangle, circle, square, triangle, circle etc. and alternates between black and white. The inner shape sequence goes: Circle, triangle, circle triangle circle etc. and alternates between white and black. Therefore, the figure that comes next must be a black triangle with an inner white circle.

Q19. B

The time on the clock is increasing by 2 hours as the sequence progresses.

Q20. A

As the sequence of the pattern has completed, it has no other option that to start the sequence again which means the lines go over themselves. The lines that make up the rectangle are growing by one each time. As the sequence of the pattern has completed, it has no other option that to start the sequence again which means the process starts again over the top of the fully drawn rectangle.

A FEW FINAL WORDS

You have now reached the end of the testing guide and no doubt you will be ready to take your abstract reasoning tests.

The majority of candidates who pass the selection process for their chosen career have a number of common attributes. These are as follows:

1. They believe in themselves.

The first factor is self-belief. Regardless of what anyone tells you, you can pass your tests and get the job that you really want. Just like any test, interview or selection process, you have to be prepared to work hard in order to be successful. Make sure you have the self-belief to pass the abstract reasoning test with high scores and fill your mind with positive thoughts.

2. They prepare fully.

The second factor is preparation. Those people who achieve in life prepare fully for every eventuality and that is what you must do when you prepare for your abstract reasoning test. Work very hard and especially concentrate on your weak areas.

3. They persevere.

Perseverance is a fantastic word. Everybody comes across obstacles or setbacks in their life, but it is what you do about those setbacks that is important. If you fail at something, then ask yourself 'why' you have failed. This will allow you to improve for next time and if you keep improving and trying, success will eventually follow. Apply this same method of thinking when you prepare for your test.

4. They are self-motivated.

How much do you want this job? Do you want it, or do you really want it?

When you apply for any job you should want it more than anything in the world. Your levels of self-motivation will shine through on your application, whilst sitting the test and also during your interview. For the weeks and months leading up to the selection process, be motivated as best you can and always keep your fitness levels up as this will serve to increase your levels of motivation.

Work hard, stay focused and be what you want...

Richard McMunn

P.S. Don't forget, you can get FREE access to more tests online at: www.PsychometricTestsOnline.co.uk

how2become

Get more books, manuals, online tests
and training courses at:

www.How2Become.com